CRUSHed

S. E. McKenzie

i

DEDICATION
To everyone who has been left out in the cold

THIS BOOK IS A BOOK OF SPECULATIVE FICTION
Characters, companies, governments, places, events, are either products of the author's imagination or used fictitiously. Any resemblance to persons (living or dead), companies, governments, places and/or events, is a coincidence and unintentional.

TABLE OF CONTENTS

CRUSHed

I

Grumpy old men; counting their cash
See the pile; had time to grow;
Opportunities from the past

Leading into tomorrow

Grumpy Old Men count their cash
In front of their window
No common sense needed

Snobocrat
The new aristocrat
Staring at Us so suspiciously

As we walk by
They tell us what it will cost to live
And what it will cost to die;

Grumpy Old Men;
Rulers of the war tone zone;
Us; we were walking through; all alone.

Going against the flow
Of Time
For they are old and cold

We are young and hot
Always looking for a bright spot
So afraid of getting shot;

Us; just a moving dot on a scatterplot;
In the war tone zone;
For it is still a rich man's world.

And we are the forgotten sons
Of Grumpy Old Men
Growing footprints in the air

If they knew Us; we are sure they would care.
But they are too busy
Growing their footprints in the air.

We are put down and never let in
And there is nothing that we can see
Their dark space has no transparency.

CRUSHed

II

Constitution; health of a nation
Born into this world
What a sensation

We are less tough when shown love;
Nowhere to go;
Just Us; locked inside this Chaos;

We all know
The power tree
Of this social ordered hierarchy

Some are put under house arrest
So they are not seen
Starving behind their locked door

The Old Way is now the New Way
Some say more true
Than ever before

Behind a locked door
Grumpy Old Men
Growing their footprints in the air.

The gap grows; we just get the glare;
We don't have a dime
Just a lot of time

No need for life's ambition
For there are no doors open to Us;
We are sneered at a lot

For we are just a moving dot
On a scatter plot
So afraid of getting shot;

While footprints grow in the air;
Manufactured fear is everywhere
Trapped inside this cosmic clock;

We are someone's forgotten son;
Our life's journey has just begun.
And we know we must stay free

For all things grow incrementally.
And confusion sets in when over-complicated baiters
Make profit as merciless haters.

CRUSHed

All about control; and we know;

We are less tough when shown love
Measuring risk
In a sensible way

Civilization
What a sensation
A bridge

Between generation
Living on this ancient world
Where Truth

Lives in every tree
So silently
Soaking in the bird's eye view

Of this Paradise
Lost; a long time ago
And we know

One day we will find
A place that we can call our own
Far away from this war tone zone.

Time
Extended for some
Stolen from others

Time

Linking the past with today
Finding a mutually beneficial way
Middle ground started to shake

We thought that we would break.

III
We are
Grumpy Old Men's forgotten sons.
And our life has just begun.

Secret meetings were all around
But Us; were never invited;
We never heard a sound.

IV
We had so little to defend;
Nothing to help Us mend.
We rose when we learned to bend.

CRUSHed

Our journey was not yet to end.

Though we were left all alone
In the War Tone Zone
Their war.

Social Impact;
Fly by Night;
We hide when there is light.

We have grown to be elastic
For Grumpy Old hair dyed men
Try to shock Us with their static

While turning our world into plastic
Imprisoned in rules written by fools
Who can only win

If they stay in position; on top of the hill;
For a level playing field
Has no such thrill

Power
Corrupts some; it is True;
And many said we were blessed

Because we were dispossessed.

So persecuted in this land of fear;
They could never love Us;
Viscous circle; spinning around

Here in this War Tone Zone

And no one could see
But Truth
And Truth lived in every tree

Flew by
As a bird's eye
In the ever changing sky

V

This fence is long
Reminding Us
That we do not belong.

Lost connection
No home
We just roam.

CRUSHed

Walking by another window
All alone
Rich women at a lingerie show

They look out and wag their finger
And our fear will always linger
Walking by windows with nowhere to hide

Our content is not known
Their life is always shown
Oh we feel so alone

As Grumpy Old Men dominate;
Control fate in secret meetings to insulate,
While they bait and hate

Their footprints are growing in the air
Above our collective head;
That is why we always feel dread

We want to live before we are dead

VI

In this fallen city, no longer pretty,
Waiting for another election
Natural Selection under their direction

Growing their footprints from the air
We are just a moving dot;
Walking on a scatter plot;

So afraid of getting shot;
They glare at us a lot;
We are young; we are hot; they are not.

We are valued way below gold
We are living in a world that is way too cold
We don't want to turn into Grumpy Old Men

Like you know who
We want to find someone to love
Someone just like you.

We want to exist
We want to be missed
Sometimes we just need a hug and kiss.

CRUSHed

Crony Capitalism
Secret process
Agenda makes them smile.

Cronies grovel for Winner's affection.
Us, we hide in this demolished section
All alone in this war tone zone.

We are just a moving dot
Walking on a scatter plot
While Grumpy Old Men

Grow their footprints from the air
Why should any of them care
They believe life can't be fair

That is probably why
They seem to always frown
Grumpy Old men always keeping Us down.

We are young so they call us trouble
We hide in the mounting dirt and rubble
In this demolished part of town; bursted bubble.

No one wants to see us around

We know the bulldozers will soon tear up the ground
For the Grumpy Old Men behind a locked door
Are selling contracts to the lowest bidder

Lower than ever before

As their footprints grow in the sky
No one cares if we live or die
We are so lonely, we could cry;

Then we look up into the sky again
We see a promise way above
We know one day there will be love

The Truth is the Lie's only fear
Illusion-making draws many near
Black hair dye and phony smile

Can only last for a little while

But the footprints growing in the sky
Could keep on growing for evermore;
While we are just a moving dot

CRUSHed

Walking all alone on a scatter plot
We are so afraid of getting shot
We are young and our blood is hot

We have nowhere that we are allowed to play
We feel so lost in this decay
But we know there could be a better way

If hate for profit would go away

Crony Capitalism
Secret process
Agenda makes them smile.

Never invited or given a clue
We are so down
We don't know what to do

And we are given nothing to see
For there is no transparency
While Grumpy Old Men

Talk endlessly

While our future waited
For their meeting, so insulated,
To end; we learned to bend; so we could mend

While the trees were taken down
One by one
The Grumpy Old Men did not know

What they had done.
Truth could see
For Truth was living

In every tree.

VII

Body Politics;
Where one still has something to give.
Body Politics;

Depends on who has the right to live.
Body politics
"Still a rich man's world"

Pre-judgmental
Pride when you are told
That the whole world is your backyard

Inheritance; pull of power;
Civilization; hiding the beast within;
Common sense; inner voice of reason;

CRUSHed

Life, water and air;
Simple things
Feed life

Time
Linking the past
Into tomorrow

We are
Grumpy Old Men's
Forgotten sons

Treated like we have an IQ of 12
No one knows where we have been
Or what we have seen.

I heard Truth cry
Not because Truth was afraid to die
But because Truth did not want

To be turned into a lie.

Crony Capitalism
Secret process
Agenda makes them smile.

Body politics
Where you learn to forgive
So the greater good can live

Have space to grow and show
A better way
For Truth could see

For Truth lived in every tree
And every tree
Gave Truth a special view

Of the power of greed;
Depravity;
Stronger force than gravity.

While Grumpy Old Men
Created an illusion
With pseudo-science to cause confusion.

CRUSHed

Black hair dye
And phony smile
That could only last a little while.

Body Politic
Illusion; Evil trick;
Poisoned air; we got so sick.

Truth is their only fear
For Truth shows the way
And was living in every Tree

So Truth could never die
For it had a bird's eye view
Of humanity

As depravity grew in strength
Depravity
Stronger than gravity

Mind of Pretense
Lacking common sense
Pretense; Loving and kind;

A promised spirit that never shows.

VIII

We wait and wait
Until today turns into tomorrow
Without love, there was so much sorrow.

In a world never our own.
We hide feelings that only fools have shown
Lost in the 'no go' section

We are told this is the way
Of natural Selection;
Body Politic; an Evil Trick;

Manufactured consent
Not caring about our content
Telling us to repent

That we have no money for rent.

Behind the darkest walls,
Still standing
In this forgotten town.

As we roam
Without a home
We steal

CRUSHed

A glimpse of humanity
Lost in all this rush
To pave the country side

Nowhere for Trees to hide
And Truth knew
For each tree gave Truth

A special view
Of humanity and depravity
Depravity; a force stronger than gravity.

We stay elastic;
For the Overlord cause so much static
As they turn our world into plastic.

Now there is nowhere to hide
For the fence keeps all the nature in
And we, called the dispossessed, out.

The rush takes over the land
No one has time to take a stand
For they all have faith in the invisible hand.

The cycle of boom and bust

Leads to our demolished part of town
Crumbling in rust
Some get trapped in artificial lust

And some say God was there to trust
For it was written all over their money
They treasured more than life itself.

The trees were taken down
One by one
During that time.

The rains began
Nowhere for the water to soak
The floods took over our part of town.

A power no one could control
Not even with a gun
So the guns were pointed at Us.

Crony Capitalism
Secret process
Agenda makes them smile.

CRUSHed

As Skulls and bones
Are hidden
Under the ground.

And we never made a fuss.
While the Grumpy Old Men
Sat around
On their make-pretend throne

There was still some space
Which could never be owned
Where life could still thrive

Beyond the rush of nine to five.

There was always hope
My Momma said to me
As she held my hand tight

The night she died
She said to me
Always keep your elasticity

And if you hold me for a little bit longer
I know that I will soon grow stronger
As the night sky turns red

Many dread
Knowing what cannot be known
Secret meetings, who knows who will show?

Grumpy Old Men, obstruct like walls
Won't be alive for much longer
And will never see

The world with less ice
Once free, the loss will be the price
The unborn will have to pay.

"When you face the world that is not your own
Remember your content
Deep inside you,"

My Momma said.
Noble Citizen; stuck between two Giants
Could get crushed; risk is hushed;

CRUSHed

Don't let them lead you to premature death
Nouveau Gestapo
March two by two

Rigid; Frigid;
As cold as Arctic ice
Fancy words to entice;

Just remember who you are
And survive the night.
Two Giants might is right;

Pulsating light shone where it could
For it was a great power of its own
So alone and misunderstood

When the light shone
Our scars, which had multiplied,
Glared for all to see.

Crony Capitalism
Secret process
Agenda makes them smile.

The Grumpy Old Men wanted it all
For they knew; soon they would no longer exist
So afraid of what they will miss

The light was in the sky
The bright atmosphere
Hidden in the darkness all around

The light could shine
But never brighten the world of fear
Even though the light was near.

We managed to get by
As the trees stood still majestically
All across our land.

That was said to be made for you and me
Owned by the crown
Not worn by the people.

As the sun faded into time
Many looked at Us
As if our existence were a crime

CRUSHed

For now we had no home
For it had been demolished
In all this rush

Very few noticed our loss
For money was the boss
And we had none

Or spoke at all
To Us in a civil tone
Yes we were all alone.

We hoped for peace
But the bulldozers came
Anyway

The demolishing continued
Without a warning
As the morning sun arose

The trees were taken down,
One by one,
They did not know what they had done.

They could not scream; they could not dream
Trees were stuffed in the wood chipper
That was over there.

The trees could not bleed
So the ground did not turn red,
Even though those trees were dead.

As the trees were crushed
One by one
They did not know what they had done.

"It was still a rich man's world,"
Or so it seems
Truth cried out loud

Crony Capitalism
Secret process
Agenda makes them smile.

There was no crowd
And no one heard
But the tree was still standing

CRUSHed

Strong and so alive
For centuries
It had survived

And seen
How mean
Ignorance had grown to be

And it was just a tree
And could not speak
About Love and Unity.

Just like Us; not our world;
Not our place
To even show our face.

"Thirty years of triple net and what did I get?"
I heard a ghostly voice ask;
Once a connected place turned into a dead end street;

While the rich kids have time to play
The day away;
The Demolishment had just begun

Crony Capitalism;
Secret process;
Agenda makes them smile.

And the Grumpy Old Men
Were now baiting
Finding new targets for hating

And we stayed elastic
Tried to avoid their static
As they turned our world

Into plastic

The great trees
Had survives wars
And strife; No longer had life.

The Sun stayed hidden
While the heavens cried
So many trees died that day

We tried to look up
And not down
For life was easier to live that way

But all we saw was the ceiling

Crony Capitalism
Secret process
Agenda makes them smile.

CRUSHed

And we had to forgive
For they did not know
What they had done.

The Overlord
Told Farmer Dan
To sell

Or he would raise hell

Until Farmer Dan
Begged for mercy
Property values be dammed

Depended on who was not seen
And who was not heard
So most of Us were treated

Bad and made Us sad.

As if we were part of a herd
And smoke filled the skies
On the other side of the hill

As our world turned to the east
It seemed as if the Sun was setting in the west
Behind the trees

All was never what it seems
But we knew soon all that was treasured
Could be lost

Staying unconcerned was best
For now; we had a place to rest
Our heads, and as we lay

We hoped for a better day.

In this world that was never ours
We remained elastic
To avoid the shock so static

The Overlords caused
While turning everything
Into plastic.

One tree escaped and would not let go
And we understood
The tree was so much more

CRUSHed

Than just a piece of wood

For we too were being torn from our ground
With very few around
To even know

We are just a moving dot
Walking on a scatter plot
So afraid of getting shot.

And the birds with the majestic wings
Were often occupied
With other things

For survival of the fittest
Became truer than ever before
As the thunder in the sky

Was hard to ignore

We stayed true
To who we were
For our content gave Us strength

And grew deep inside Us.

Not to be hidden behind a locked door;
For we had no door
The same old story from a time before.

If we spoke
Or were seen
We could be baited for we were hated.

So we hide our face, as we roamed from place to place
For our status
Defined who we were now

Would we find Paradise Lost?
The cost?
Weapons molded into plowshares

It would take a lot of love
Not needed in any back room
Where the process of gloom and doom

Is glorified
We knew something important
Had to be revived

CRUSHed

A place where we could still find trees
For shade
To hide from the glare

Of Pre-judgmental culture
Blinded to discrimination;
Against the young and nature.

And those without means
A harsh world
As Crony Capitalism

System of convenience
Takes hold
Value oil and gold

More than water and air
Unconsciously designing fate
Of Hate and waste.

You can't speak to stakeholders beneath;
Now Skulls and bones; Process of exhaustion
And wealth depletion

Before our life began
We shared Rights of Man;
To live in dignity; beyond an economy hidden in a drawer.

While rich men count their stash of cash
Their guarded eye looks out their window
Onto a Public sidewalk; called their backyard.

Slayers;
Social speculators;
Accidents; Professional Degraders;

Decided where obstacles would be placed
Whenever a certain face
Was seen

God knew
Some said
A place between nature and the unknown stream;

Unified less reason to scream;
So many trees had died
Stakeholders; without a voice there is no choice;

But one little tree stood out all alone.

CRUSHed

And Truth had a bird's eye view
And could see
From every tree

Greed; Depravity
A force
Stronger than gravity.

And the secret deciders
Could not see outside their door
For they were hiders.

Truth could see
For Truth lived in every tree
And each bird had grown to be

Truth's eye
So Truth had a greater chance to spread
Before being turned into a lie

As Grumpy Old Men
Hid behind a locked door
They used illusion and confusion

Black hair dye and a phony smile
That would only last a while
So the Overlords were in a hurry

To get all they could.

But they could not see the ice
Melting from the Mountain above.
And we all knew

We needed a home; a place to grow love;
We just needed a bit of land; that would be enough;
And we would need nothing more;

Just a small plot, for our roots to cling to.

As the roads took over the land
In places never mapped before
All the decisions were made

Behind a locked door
While Grumpy Old Men
Black hair dye and phony smile

CRUSHed

Used illusion, confusion
And called it fate;
We hoped it would not be too late

As Grumpy Old Men fell asleep; hidden;
Behind a locked door
Now in control of every power meter in the land

Their gain, our pain;
Professional complainers,
In a process that was secret they said for privacy's sake

But Truth could see
That all they did while they hid
Was waiting for their pay-day

And their love for money and the power
To monopolize
Paved their path to glory;

Still fooled by their first mistake
They did not know what they had done
While smoke and mirrors blocked

And magnified the sun.

And Nature's beauty; a work not yet complete;
Was fenced in
To only be enjoyed by the elite.

This was the new way; once the old way
As the highway needed more lanes
We grew to be elastic

So we could avoid the Overlords static
As they turned our world
Into plastic.

The Overlords said this was best
For all living creatures
Needing to eat and nest.

And Truth cried
For Truth had a bird's eye view
Could see from every tree

Greed; depravity;
Stronger force than gravity
As the Grumpy Old Men

CRUSHed

Took all they could
Behind a locked door
That led to many more

Created illusion
Pseudo-science and confusion
Behind black hair dye and phony smile

Still, they would only be living for a while
And Truth cried
For truth did not want to be turned into a lie.

As it rained
The rivers began to flow beyond their banks
For the water was living

Everyone knew
That the Overlords
Would sell the water and air too

If they only could.
Us; we were trapped in this cosmic clock;
Where Opportunity never knocks.

The Overlords captured the stream
On paper during a meeting
Behind a locked door

We could only scream or dream
Or begin the search for a better world
While the old way became the new way.

We saw a hammer in the sky
And we knew we weren't alone
For the power of life

Was still everywhere.
We too were stakeholders
Sharing this common ground

Civilization?
A word
To cause sensation.

Divide and conquer
Was the Overlord's way
Just another Fear Tactic

CRUSHed

Sometimes could cause Panic
While the Overlords
Were busy turning our world into plastic.

Our birthright
To live and exist
Was greatly missed

For the old way became the new way
And it was still a rich man's world
Or so it seemed.

Still, we could feel all this wild life
Pulsate through Us
Not yet the chosen ones

Still Earth's
Forgotten sons
Hanging on the best we can.

And one tree stood tall
And watched it all;
Its destiny was to fall.

The passersby gave Us a dirty look
For the beauty in our demolished
Part of town; was gone

And left Us in manufactured slums
Many called Us bums;
For now we had nothing to maintain

And our faces grew scarred with pain.

IX

The big machines dig for oil
Replacing humans with their toil
One task jobs without design

No negotiating
With bionic tone
Fear the mechanical

For you are alone
Don't Search for Paradise lost
For it has been sold

At an undisclosed cost.
Ethical thinking
Good or bad

CRUSHed

When the harm cannot be reversed
Humanity has been cursed
By those living in a time

So long ago
Mean spirit lingered on
Above the ground

Skulls and bones lay beneath

X
Superior orders
From above
Don't call it love

As the rain came down in torrents
And could not soak into the ground
And the floods grew; we knew

For the trees and their root systems

Had been demolished
Inside a wood chipper
What took centuries to grow

Was destroyed so quick

We knew our hope
Depended on calm
We froze to avoid feeling our alarm

The spirit roamed in time
Never finding peace
For he was not made that way.

No one to blame
We had to play the game
To live in balance and harmony

On the land
Not just on
A pile of money

XI

We thanked the power we could not understand
For it seemed to have given Us a hand
Even when the demolishers were in command

CRUSHed

For they too needed water and air
Which made the struggle
A little more fair

Since the Overlords had to care

We are so alone
Walking in the War Tone Zone
We are the forgotten sons

Of Grumpy Old Men
Planning it all
Behind a wall

Growing their footprints in the sky.
We are just a moving dot
Walking through a scatter plot

So afraid of getting shot.

The winds came;
More trees broke and fell
We knew we were living

In a man-made hell.
We were able to find someone kind
In the most demolished part of town.

We watched; having no say;
As our world changed before our eyes;
We did what we could;

In the world that was dominated
By Grumpy Old Men who baited,
In secret meetings so insulated

While growing their footprints in the air.

We are just a moving dot
Walking on a scatter plot
So afraid of getting shot.

Our lives on hold; Still not old;
We have passed the test
Of manufactured distress

By overcoming our duress
Staying numb under stress
While Truth lives in every tree

CRUSHed

Watching over you and me;
It had a bird's eye view
Over all Humanity.

While Grumpy Old men dissolve privacy
Wanting control over all Destiny
Denying their threat over democracy;

Grumpy Old Men destined to die
Turned Truth's voice
Into a lie

For Truth was what is and what was,
Evidence behind that locked door,
Hidden so no one knew.

"And without you, sweet birds,
I would be so alone
Hiding in these shadows

Always out of view."

I heard Truth take a breath and continue to say,
"I see Depravity growing all around
Stronger force than gravity holding onto the ground.

Evil in disguise
Hate softens
What should make a person cry.

Greed justifies so much waste
Consuming in too much haste
Transforming destiny

Into a place more hostile
Harder to smile
Or want to linger for a while.

By design
Man-made hell
Needed struggle; don't give up the fight

For what we all knew is right.

There were many ghosts
Lost without a name;
They were not to blame.

Only a voice
Could leave a plea;
So that one day

CRUSHed

We would see
The power of True Love
Growing across this land.

The birds with majestic wings
Needed very little
For they had their own way

And Truth could see
From every tree
And was waiting silently;

To feed; while humans
Were left dying
In all this greed.

For their hands were tied
Behind their back
Planning another attack

Growing their footprints
From the air;
While baiting and hating

We knew we had to stay elastic
To avoid the static
A mind-war fear tactic

While the Overlords
Turned our world into plastic
Bones and skulls below our Earth

Wanted their power back.

And the power hungry
Politician
Told the farmer to give up his land

For farmland spoiled his view
When playing golf
As the ball

Rolled down
An artificially green hill
Just for a thrill

The land was taken out of food production.

The farmer said no
The politician said go
For the farmer was said to be spoiling the view

CRUSHed

"We control the rise and fall
Of property value
Not you,"

The Overlord said.
"You must not be seen
Nor heard

Our power of inheritance
Makes Us who we are"
And Truth cried

Truth could see
Humanity from every tree.
Greed; Depravity;

Stronger Force than Gravity.
As Grumpy Old Men
Hid behind illusion

Black hair dye and confusion.
And unethical legalist said
'Our might is right."

We are behind this locked door
We are safe here; nothing to fear;
As he began to memorize rule after rule,

Victimizing Us with his projection.

Truth began to cry
Didn't want to be turned
Into another lie.

And Truth had a bird's eye view;
For Truth could see
From every tree.

And knew
The old way was not new
Unethical Legalist; just another fool;

Still a rich man's world; So cruel;
Mind of Pretense; lacking common sense;
Truth could see and cried

Did not want to be turned
Into a lie
While watching every tree die.

CRUSHed

XII

We knew the game
We had to play
For the Overlords had nothing new to say.

We stayed elastic
To avoid the static
While the Overlord turned everything into plastic.

The birds with majestic wings
Helped Us think of noble things
Though some were caught in the fences

That were all around
Many were able to fly away
Giving Us strength

To face a new day

The birds with majestic wings
Saw what could never be spoken
While our pain had been awoken.

Our privacy
Our boundaries
Everything we knew

Was under vicious attack
By the baiters, the haters
And the property value inflators

Planned behind closed doors
For the truth
Would take years to show.

Us; the young were still elastic.
More able to recover from the Overlord's static;
While they turned our world into plastic.

Once truth grew visible, the Overlords
Would no longer exist nor be
Still we would never be free

For the Overlords would remain in memory

Paying the debt was always delayed
Waiting for the day the Overlords would fade way
Into the past.

And their debt would be left behind
For Us to repay
For we were the generation born into doom

CRUSHed

And often we forgot the flowers that bloom
Freely
In this world of gloom

We followed the sign
Promising to see
The best place in the world

But that place could no longer be
For the Tree of Unity
Had gone missing.

XIII

We searched anyway
For we all agreed
That Paradise lost must be found

So we searched for that place
Promised to Us
A long time ago

While rich men count their cash
In front of their window
No common sense is needed

Hiding the beast within; Snobocrat;
The new aristocrat
They will hate you, if they hate your hat.

Some have guns
Not knowing creates
A state of runs.

We looked on the ground
For tracks; a path to follow;
Which may lead Us to our Promised Land.

It was said to be

A place of peace and love
Sheltered by mountains on all sides
A place where we would all belong

We followed the Path
And to our dismay
We found what we were looking for

Blocking our way

CRUSHed

The Tree of Unity had taken root;
And was sharing our air;
So we made the rule

To never be a tool for a fool
Or let our Tree of Unity be sold
For paper or gold.

In a land of boom and bust
Everything we knew had turned to rust
Except our love, except our trust;

We hugged Tree of Unity
And then each other.
We called our neighbors

Sister and Brother.
And as we held hands
We felt a glow beginning to flow;

No more excuses to discriminate
And agitate;
Or poison the world with hate.

Across foreign lands
We watched as the Overlords
Dropped their guns.

And a new era had begun;
And what a wonderful world
It was.

THE END

Produced by S.E. McKenzie Productions
First Print Edition August 2015

Enquiries: 1(778)992-2453
Mailing Address:
S. E. McKenzie Productions
168 B 5th St.
Courtenay, BC
V9N 1J4

Email Address:
messidartha@aol.com

http://www.amazon.com/SarahMcKenzie/e/B00H9RWX48/ref=ntt
_dp_epwbk_0

www.ingramcontent.com/pod-product-compliance
Lightning Source LLC
Chambersburg PA
CBHW060536030426
42337CB00021B/4299